Everything
I KNOW
ABOUT MEN
I learnt from my dog

CLARE STAPLES

With a foreword by Candace Bushnell, author of Sex and the City

Crombie Jardine
PUBLISHING LIMITED

www.crombiejardine.com

This edition was first published by
Crombie Jardine Publishing Limited in 2005

Copyright © 2005, Clare Staples

ISBN: 1-905102-25-9

Photographs: Helena Burton

All photographs have been reproduced with the kind permission of the author.

Design: www.glensaville.com

Printed and bound in Belgium by Proost

For Paul . . . who taught me unconditional love.

Mr. Big

THANKS TO

Robert Kirby, Candace Bushnell, Michael Neill, Neil Reading,
Helena Burton, Dougray Scott, Elle Macpherson, Simon Cowell,
Andrew Neil, Adrian Gill, Sacha Gervasi, Alexa Pearmund,
Catriona Jardine, David Crombie, Glen Saville, Trevor Leighton,
Nicky Clarke, Paul Duddridge, Dinny at AllDog, Mum,
AA, HP, LG, Mr. Big.

And all the men I have dated who behaved like dogs . . . only worse.

One day I would like to be the person my dog thinks I am.

Anon

Foreword by Candace Bushnell

This wonderfully clever book is the work of my very dear friend, Clare Staples.

I met Clare years ago in London, and I always thought of her as the English version of a Sex and the City girl. She was (and still is) beautiful, smart and sexy, and we had many memorable evenings not just in London but around the world. Of course, like a true Sex and the City girl, Clare had her share of romantic ups and downs, all of which we discussed endlessly. One of my favourite memories is the time we irritated an entire planeload of people on Virgin Atlantic by talking loudly about men and their deficiencies. By the time we arrived in New York, we'd come to the conclusion that the only way to deal with men was to train them. Like dogs. I'd like to think that it was during that transatlantic flight that the idea for this book was born.

When Clare gave me a prototype for this, I found it utterly charming and absolutely spot-on. The truth is that we do often compare men to dogs, and the language of dogs seems to be one that men are instinctively familiar with. How many times have you heard one man describe another as 'a dog'? Note that this is not usually an insult, but is often said with envy and even admiration.

By the simple act of comparing men to dogs, Clare Staples has achieved what a hundred years of psychology and self-help books haven't: she has finally made the male sex *comprehensible*.

CONTENTS

INTRODUCTION

When I got Mr. Big as a puppy, I immediately started doing all the things suggested in my puppy books regarding training and discipline. I took him to puppy classes when he was old enough, read more books and scoured the internet for clues about how to get him to do what I wanted.

However, when we got to the park and I undid his lead, he was off after everything that looked more interesting than me. I tried calling him, yelling at him, waving, using every tone of voice I knew and still I couldn't get him to pay the blindest bit of notice. I started taking treats to the park to bribe him to come back to me. Sometimes this worked but often it didn't.

One day it was wet and windy and cold. I had been calling Mr. Big for so long my

voice was hoarse. Then something just snapped. I turned on my heel and started walking home alone. I didn't care if he came with me or not. I was over him. I had had enough. I was five minutes away when I heard the sound of a dog running behind me. I carried on. He slid to a stop beside me and looked up at my face with such fear, contrition and – yes, finally! – submission in his eyes that I was amazed. On our way home, he walked to heel, perfectly in step with me and it crossed my mind how like men dogs are: show them any interest and they take off; ignore them and they try everything to get your attention. Treat them well and they take you for granted, treat them mean and . . . well, you know the rest.

So I continued to train Mr. Big and found that he responded particularly well to certain tactics. Little by little I realized that the same techniques I was using with Mr. Big applied to men as well. I could see as clearly as anything that there was really no difference at all between men and dogs when it came to natural instincts and behaviour.

They say man's best friend is his dog and it is not really surprising when you look at the similarities between the two. I have spent years discussing, analysing and dissecting the behaviour of various men with wonderful girlfriends, especially Candace, and I realize just how much I have learnt over time and how much is relevant to both species. After reading this book I don't think you will be able to look at either men or dogs in the same way as before and if you follow my tips I guarantee your relationships with both will be more successful. . .

Good luck!

SELECTING A BREED

Pick your man carefully. As a general rule avoid addicts, commitment-phobic emotionally-unavailable angry men, married ones, liars, narcissists, Scorpios and actors.

CHOOSING A DOG

There are many hundreds of different kinds of dogs to choose from. Hunt around for a dog that suits you and your lifestyle. It is very important to pick one that fits into your daily routine. Find one that appears bright, alert and healthy. Don't, whatever you do, just take the first one that comes along. Make sure you are compatible: your new dog will be a big part of your life and you may well be spending the next ten years with him.

Don't date a slob. No matter how good a man's heart is or what a great guy he seems, if he looks a mess, most likely he is a mess. A man who takes pride in his appearance has self-worth and that is a great quality.

SELF-WORTH

Make sure your dog is groomed regularly. Dogs have a lot of pride and are inherently vain, sometimes even narcissistic animals. Their appearance is very important to them and they look to you to keep them at their best; apart from licking the parts they can reach they are unable to do much more in the way of making themselves beautiful.

Handsome men are never a great bet. Often they have learnt to rely on their looks and as a result have not had to develop a personality or sense of humour – two far more important qualities. What's inside his head, heart and soul matter much more. A vain and self-obsessed man will quickly become very unattractive as a partner.

LOOKS

Don't choose a dog for his looks alone. People who do that are usually incredibly insecure and just want a pet to make them look good. Remember that looks are only surface deep – loyalty, devotion, an eagerness to please and unconditional love truly are the most wonderful things you can ever experience from your dog and they are far more important than the colour of his eyes or the softness of his coat. And of course it goes without saying that a handsome dog is far more likely to stray.

Dating older men is tricky: they are less malleable and more stuck in their ways. Be cautious of a man over forty who has never been married or made an emotionally mature commitment. However, find a man who is keen to learn and he will be like putty in your hands. It really is never too late to start anything, even being a good man.

OLD DOG, NEW TRICKS

It is true what they say about it being hard to teach an old dog new tricks but it's not impossible. If you didn't get your dog as a puppy, but rather as a mature dog, it will be harder to change his ways. Once a dog has realized what he can get away with when he's had a weak owner he will always try it on with you. You will need a lot of patience but stand your ground.

Pay particular attention to how a new man in your life changes when he drinks. If you notice he becomes more aggressive, turns into an idiot, starts flirting with every woman in sight or becomes sarcastic and belittling toward you, get rid of him.

DRINKING

It is very important for you to watch what your dog drinks. Some breeds of dog are prone to a serious condition called bloat. This causes the dog's belly to swell to a huge size and if not caught quickly can cause death. Many experts believe that a huge contributory factor to this is drinking too much too fast, but stress is also to blame. Be extremely vigilant around your dog's drinking habits.

It is important to see early on what a man's attitude is to children. Take note if he winces at the sound of a baby crying or avoids going anywhere he might encounter these little creatures. If a man tells you he doesn't want a committed relationship, marriage or children and you do, he is just not the one for you.

KIDS

When choosing a dog, make sure you pick one that is good with children. Even if you don't have kids, or any plans to have them, you will invariably encounter them everywhere. Children, especially when they are very small, are easy to scare and easy to knock over and you should teach your dog early on not to do either. When he's a puppy and you are out where there are little ones, let babies and toddlers pet him as much as they want. Speak gently, reassure your dog that children are safe and nothing to be scared of and he will realize they are bundles of fun and not something to be avoided.

"

If a dog will not come to you after having looked you in the face, you should go home and examine your conscience.

Woodrow Wilson

"

IN THE BEGINNING

When you first meet a man who is potential dating material, make and keep in mind your three absolute 'no exceptions' for a boyfriend. Mine are that he must be financially manageable, have a sense of humour and be consistent.

NO EXCEPTIONS

When you start training your dog there are a lot of things for him to learn so it is a good idea to have three bottom line NOs that you enforce no matter what. For Mr. Big these were: no sleeping on the bed, no jumping up on people, and no eating people's food. Enforcing these rules from the very beginning will make your life a lot easier later on.

Set the rules of your relationship early on. Things like calling when he says he will, paying for dates, bringing you little presents, taking you out to romantic places . . . Teach him the requirements of your relationship and don't reward him with anything until he has learnt these simple ground rules.

TRAINING

As soon as you bring your dog home, start teaching him what is good behaviour and what is not. All dogs must be trained from day one that you are the boss. Dogs instinctively want to earn the pack leader's approval. Make the house rules early on in the relationship and it will be easier to enforce them. Dogs like rules; they bring structure and security and dogs don't really want to think of you as a pushover anyway, even though they may quite often test the boundaries to see where they are. It is part of a dog's nature to try to get away with as much as he can and it is your job to stop him.

When you first meet your man don't change anything for him. Don't give up your friends or hobbies. Never cancel anything to be with him. Even when you are full of fear that he will never ask you out again, stay strong and tell him you already have plans.

ROUTINE

Don't change your life for your dog. Keep doing all the things you did before; your dog has to fit into your life, not the other way around. When you first get a dog, the chances are he will whine when you leave him alone but he'll soon get used to it and appreciate you more when you spend quality time with him.

When you first meet him, don't smother your man. It is the worst thing you can do. Don't get in his space, in his face or in his being-by-myself place. Give him plenty of room to be himself and don't try and corner him or cage him. Ever.

SMOTHERING

Dogs thrive on affection but always let your dog come to you for attention and cuddles, unless you're rewarding him for good behaviour. Neediness makes dogs uncomfortable. So when you feel in need of emotional support, call a girlfriend and go and spend an evening with her instead. When you come home, your dog will be so happy to see you again it's a joy.

In the early stages of a relationship, disappear occasionally and don't explain where you have been. Give the impression you have an exciting and interesting life away from him. He will instinctively fight to spend more time with you.

SCARE HIM

Dogs learn well by being a little scared. Sometimes, if a dog doesn't do what you ask him, hide behind a tree and watch him. To start with he won't be too worried and will go about his business with confidence. He'll go to see other dogs, sniff a few trees, paddle in the pond, thoroughly enjoy his freedom, safe in the knowledge that you are there watching and waiting. However, if he suddenly looks around and realizes he cannot see you he'll panic. Leave him for a few more seconds, then emerge and call him. He'll run over, totally delirious to see you again.

If you want a long term relationship don't sleep with a man until you have dated him for four weeks. Firstly because that is how long it takes to get to know a man enough to decide if he is for you and secondly because holding out is the best way to ensure seeing him again.

GET TO KNOW YOUR DOG

When you have chosen a breed and found a litter spend time getting to know your puppy before you take it home. Even at a very early age puppies have a personality. Choose a puppy that isn't the most boisterous and playful but also is not the quietest and most subdued. It is very important that you make sure you can return the dog within a four week period in case you don't get along.

"

To err is human,
to forgive, canine.

Unknown

"

ABOUT YOUR PET

Men are genetically programmed to be hunter-gatherers. They like to pursue things and the harder the things are to catch the more valued they become. Don't be too easy. Be elusive and flighty and men will go to any lengths to possess you.

UNAVAILABILITY

All dogs want what they can't have. When Mr. Big was a puppy, he got hold of the cleaning lady's feather duster one day. He loved it and managed to pull out half the feathers before she could retrieve it. After that we always made sure that it was safely out of his reach but he will still stare up at it for hours and try to get it off her whenever she is using it. He only wants it because it is unattainable. It is his Holy Grail.

Don't even try to read or worry about the mood your man is in. Men have more moods than there are names for. It is imposssible to predict them or to understand them. Just carry on regardless and don't let his mood affect yours.

MOODS

A dog has four moods – happy, sad, cross and concentrating*.
It is important you are able to read your dog's moods so that you
can slightly adjust your behaviour accordingly. Happy: you might find
this contagious, so be happy too. Sad: be extra nice to him and give him
a treat or take him for a long walk. Cross: give him his space and don't
take it personally. Concentrating: just try not to laugh.

* From The Curious Incident of the Dog in the Night-Time.

Men are not the fearless hunks that we have been led to believe. Most men have had their hearts broken, felt stupid, and had bad relationships that scarred them and left them scared. So when their feelings get hurt or you touch an old wound, be understanding and don't push his buttons just because you can.

FEAR

Most dogs suffer from some level of fear-based aggression. They want you to think that they are big and strong and brave and tough but the truth is that inside they are really quite frightened of most things. Especially things they don't understand or are unfamiliar with. More often than not a dog will bark the loudest when he is the most scared – not because he is angry or vicious. Knowing that really helps and all you need to do is allay his fear with a stroke and an encouraging word and he will be fine again.

When he is around others, let your man be a man. Men judge other men and decide on their status by three things: physical size, wealth and the woman by their side. Don't criticize, belittle or be sarcastic to your man in front of anyone.

ALPHA MALE

A dog needs to think he is top dog. When he is around other dogs, he doesn't want them to know that he has an owner and boss. There will be a lot of sniffing and posturing while dogs size each other up and decide who is dominant. This is all part and parcel of being a dog, so let him get on with it. When the challenge is over, make a fuss of him, tell him how fine and brave he is. The only time to act is when it looks as if there might be a fight – then just walk away or cause a distraction. Never get between two fighting dogs.

All men can be very annoying. There isn't a man on the planet who isn't and who won't drive you mad sometimes with his completely incomprehensible and bizarre behaviour. When it gets particularly bad take some space. Make a list of all the things that make you crazy about him, not with him.

OFF DAYS

All dogs will drive you crazy occasionally. Some days your dog won't do a thing you want him to and everything he does will irritate you. You may honestly feel as though you cannot stand the sight of him and would like to get rid of him. Then this passes and you look at his furry face. He pads over and puts his head in your lap and looks up at you and you feel as though your heart could burst, you love him so much. He's your best friend, he makes you laugh, he's kind and sweet, big-hearted and full of love and nothing could replace him. Everybody has off days but they pass and you quickly remember why you love your dog and why he loves you.

The dog is a gentleman;
I hope to go to his heaven
not man's.

Mark Twain

MAINTAINING YOUR RELATIONSHIP

Give your man space. Men hate feeling trapped or fenced in. They think they want their space so give it to them. The strangest thing is that when you give it to them without them asking, they want exactly the opposite.

SOCIALIZING

Dogs need to socialize. They like to go off and meet other dogs but will always come back to you if you let them have their space. If you call your dog endlessly or resort to going over to get him, he'll run away or sulk. Give him his freedom and he'll very quickly get bored and start worrying about where you are.

Cook for him once a week and make sure his favourite snacks are in your cupboard. If you can't cook, get a friend to teach you how to make a perfect meal and practise it a few times before you make it for him.

FEEDING

Dogs love their food. Make sure that you are the one who feeds your dog the most. It is very true that the way to a dog's heart is through his stomach. Many people think that a dog's main urge is sexual but in fact science has proven that it is actually hunger. When your dog realizes that you are the main provider of all the good things he eats, he will never leave you for another.

Men can hurt you . . . badly. Emotional pain can be worse than physical pain. Watch for red flags and make a note of them so you stay out of fantasy and in reality. When you hear alarm bells, don't mistake them for wedding bells. It is much easier to get out sooner rather than later.

BEWARE

Be very careful about rough-housing with your dog especially when he is large. I have been caught off guard twice when I haven't been paying enough attention and as a result have suffered a cracked jaw and cracked rib by being knocked over. When walking your dog always concentrate and be aware . . . it is better to spot and thus avoid a potential problem than have to sort out the consequences after the event.

Most women tend to get their self-worth from relationships (big mistake); men get it from their work. Don't compete with his work or the amount of time he spends on it: a man needs his work in order to feel good about himself and that will make him a happier and nicer person to be around.

WORK

Dogs love projects and take them very seriously. These can include gnawing a bone, chasing a bird, digging a hole, searching for food and shaking a toy. They are all approached with the same serious intent and given the same importance. When your dog is wrapped up in a project, and momentarily forgets all about you, don't take it personally. He still loves you, regardless of his temporary distractions.

Be the one to suggest nights off. Tell him you're busy before he tells you he is. Make plans with your friends and then suggest that he goes out with his friends or catches a film. Always be the one to make alternative plans and never break them for him even if he asks you to.

REJECTION

Reject him before he rejects you. When you get to the park with your dog, always make sure that you send him away before he goes by himself. Get your dog to sit, then unclip his lead and tell him to go off and play by pointing to the distance and saying, 'Go on'. This serves to reinforce who is in control and makes his fun time your idea, not his. That way he will associate his good times with you and only you.

If you eliminate smoking and gambling, you will be amazed to find that almost all an Englishman's pleasures can be, and mostly are, shared by his dog.

George Bernard Shaw

REWARD AND PUNISHMENT

When your man does something that you like – for example brings you a present, takes you somewhere special or does something that requires thought and effort – reward him. Give him a treat, spoil him, make him feel like a god. Give his ego a good stroking and he will unconsciously associate his behaviour with the reward and do it again.

POSITIVE REINFORCEMENT

All dogs love to be praised. Train a dog with positive rewards for positive behaviour and never smack a dog for behaving badly. If you shout at a dog, he will associate the scolding not with his own bad behaviour but with you instead. As a result he will become fearful of you, start to distance himself and generally see you as a source of discomfort or pain. Praise and stroke your dog when he is good, even if he is just walking well beside you. He will then adore you and see you as the source of good feelings and love.

Even though it is important to give your man his space, he needs to know what you will and will not tolerate. If his behaviour occasionally causes concern, you may well have to re-establish the basic ground rules. Once your trust has been restored, you will feel happier about letting him run free again.

LEAD

All dogs need to be put on a lead sometimes. Use a retractable one: it is more flexible and allows your dog to have his space from you when you are out and about. However, it also gives you the option of reining him in and putting him on a short lead when there is any danger of him behaving badly.

When you need to get your man to do something he doesn't enjoy – like going shopping with you, or taking the rubbish out – simply distract him with thoughts or promises of things he does like. Before you know it the chore will be done.

DISTRACTION

Dogs are easily distracted. Get your dog to do something he doesn't like by distracting him with something he does like. Then immediately give him his favourite treat and he will quickly forget all about the chore. When giving your dog his bath, for example, take along a few of his favourite toys or a snack. Quickly wash and shampoo him whilst he is busy thinking about his treat.

When your man does something you don't like or is disrespectful or neglectful, the only way he will learn not to do it again is for you to withdraw. Do not take his calls, answer his texts or make plans to see him.

NAUGHTINESS

Dogs hate being ignored. If your dog behaves badly, the best way to teach him this will not be tolerated is to simply ignore him. Act completely uninterested in him and don't make eye contact. Busy yourself by doing other things and he will try harder and harder to get your attention. Ultimately, he will resort to dropping his favourite toys in your lap as a way of saying sorry. When this happens, pat his head and give him a kiss; his relief will make him think long and hard before doing that again.

A lot of negative qualities in men can be caused by their own insecurities. You can only do so much to try and help them feel better. In the end they have to learn to love themselves; you can't do it for them. If the consequences of their low self-worth start making you feel worthless, then it's time to call it a day.

SECURITY

Dogs can suffer from poor self-image and low self-worth, exactly like humans. With so much cross-breeding there are quite a lot of mutts walking around with the body of one breed and the head of another and you know just by looking at them that they can tell something isn't right. But they are still beautiful in somebody's eyes. Help to bolster your dog's self-esteem with lots of praise and affection. Love him until he learns to love himself.

Man is a dog's idea of
what God should be.

Holbrook Jackson

HOW TO STAY THE BOSS

Don't call your man, text him or turn up at his house unexpectedly no matter what. Let him do the chasing. Always end the call or visit before he does; you want to have him feeling as though you are always slightly out of his reach.

LET HIM BE

If you chase a dog, it will run away. This is always true, no matter what. The more you chase, the more he will run. There is just something in his nature that makes him do this no matter how much he loves you and how much he loves being with you. A dog instinctively becomes nervous when stalked and chased. However, turn your back on him and walk away quickly and he will come running after you, determined to catch up with you and be by your side.

Right from the start, tell him you need time to see your friends and keep up with your old life. Encourage him to do the same and have boys' nights out. You are not threatened by anything or anyone.

PLAY TIME

Dogs need to play and occasionally they will get caught up in a really fun game. Your dog might have found some others to play with, a squirrel to chase, or just a really good smell that needs further investigation. During these periods, regardless of the fact that he loves you completely, he will forget about you. He will hear the sound of your voice calling him but it will just seem unimportant, annoying even. When he finally comes back to you, the worst thing you can do is be angry. He is back, so greet him with enthusiasm and a big pat and remind him how good it is to be with you.

Do not show your man you are that distressed when he is leaving. Any signs of clinginess, overt dependency or neediness are the ultimate turn-off. You have your own life which should be full of other things apart from him. It is a mistake to depend on anyone except yourself. You are the only one who can make you happy.

SEPARATION ANXIETY

This is a common condition with many dogs and one you need to deal with promptly. The dog's fear of being alone will manifest itself in a variety of ways: destructive behaviour within seconds of your departure; howling, whining, barking, depression or even aggression at any sign of your leaving; and excessive greeting when you return. This is caused by an over-dependence on a human being and is distressing for both dog and owner. The best way to deal with it is by de-sensitization – leaving the dog for very short periods quite often, gradually extending each time away until the dog is reassured you will always be back.

If your man shows the slightest sign of aggression towards you, show him the door immediately. If you let him get away with it even once, he will do it again and the behaviour will always get worse. There is no justification for violence from a man.

AGGRESSION

Do not tolerate any aggression towards you from your dog. If he growls directly at you, bares his teeth or actually bites you then get rid of him. I don't mean put him down but I do mean let him go to a new home with someone who can handle difficult dogs. You and he might not be compatible, but there will be someone out there who will be able to love him and tame him. It doesn't have to be you.

When your man calls or comes over to see you, don't ever, ever be too excited to hear from him or see him. Tell him you'll call him back or when he comes over, finish doing whatever you were doing. Make him wait for you and always give him the impression that he is not the most important thing in your life. He never should be.

SUPERIORITY

As in a pack of wolves, there is a pecking order surrounding the 'top dog'. Being aloof and in power elevates the leader from the lesser dogs. Don't fuss too much over your dog and don't ever bow down to him or he will get ideas above his station and will be impossible to control.

The more people I meet,
the more I like my dog.

Unknown

SEXUAL BEHAVIOUR

Don't be afraid to explore where he enjoys being kissed the most. Try nuzzling his ears and neck for starters. This can immobilize a grown man. Once you have found his special spot, take advantage of it whenever you need to.

SWEET SPOT

All dogs have a sweet spot – you just have to find it. Most dogs love their ears being rubbed or having their bottom scratched, just above the tail. Give your dog a good scratch there and he won't even be able to move he'll be in such ecstasy. Sometimes your dog will come to you hoping for a good scratch, sometimes you'll give him one and sometimes not. The trick is to keep him guessing but when you do give him one make sure it feels really good!

If you are dating a man who is incapable of keeping it in his trousers, has no understanding of the concept of loyalty or fidelity, and consistently humiliates and embarrasses you, then end the relationship! If you don't, you are signing up for a lifetime of jealousy and insecurity that will erode your self-worth. Kick him to the curb fast.

SEX

What do you do if your dog is very highly sexed and starts trying to mount everything in sight? Try to distract him. However, if the problem persists, you may well have to resort to castration. In the long run it is kinder to the dog as it gets rids of the embarrassing social behaviour for him. You will also find that it gives you added peace of mind about him straying or becoming aggressive.

Don't flirt with anyone in front of your man or tell him how many other men are crazy about you. Assume that he realizes how desirable you are. If someone flirts with you when you are with your man, simply pay more attention to your man than usual. Your loyalty will be rewarded.

INSECURITY

All dogs get a little jealous and insecure around other dogs, particularly if you pet or pay too much attention to the others. Yours will not like you coming home smelling of another dog: it will make him worry about where you are when he's not with you. If you are too friendly with another dog, yours will probably feel threatened, bare his teeth and growl, which is not nice for you or him. When another dog comes up to you and yours, simply say hello and pat him on the head briefly. Then turn back to your dog and give him a nice stroke to reassure him that he is still your favourite.

You will know pretty quickly what does it for him; that thing you do that drives him crazy and renders him speechless and makes him whimper. When you know what it is, don't do it again for a while. Hold back and he'll be unable to think about anything else.

TREATS

Dogs love treats but an occasional, surprise treat is a lot more fun than an expected daily one. No matter how much he loves a bone or stick of beef jerky, if your dog gets it every day it will begin to lose its special appeal. A treat given to reward particularly good behaviour will be valued and your dog will be more inclined to behave well again in the hope of getting another delicacy. Dogs, however dumb, quickly start to associate good behaviour with treats; it's the best and most painless way to train them. They respond very well to bribery and best of all they don't even realize that they are being manipulated.

Boys will be boys and although we would prefer the man of our dreams to be faithful and monogamous, it isn't very likely. If your man loves you, and his lapses are very few and far between, then it is better to turn a blind eye, as long as he's discreet and respectful towards you. It really does mean nothing at all to a man.

DOGS WILL BE DOGS

Your dog will love you unconditionally, with all his big heart. You are, after all, the most important thing in his life. However, occasionally he will smell a bitch on heat across the park and you'll be forgotten for one crazy moment; some urges are just too strong. He doesn't have the capacity or intelligence to stop and rationalize his behaviour and how it might affect you. He'll be off, without worrying about the consequences. When he finds her, nature may well take its course but you should stand safe in the knowledge that the moment it's all over he'll want to find you, love you, come home with you and most likely never think about that bitch again.

No man can be condemned for owning a dog. As long as he has a dog, he has a friend; and the poorer he gets, the better friend he has.

Will Rogers

IN CONCLUSION

The secret, magic ingredient to all this is confidence. This is irresistible, intoxicating and hugely attractive to both men and dogs. If you don't feel confident, then act as if you do and you soon will. Men and dogs have the uncanny ability to smell fear and both creatures will instinctively take advantage of it when they sense it in you.

I have spent a long time studying both good and bad relationships, men and dogs. I learnt most lessons the hard way, but whenever I messed up in a relationship,

I always took away something useful. The key thing to remember is that if you don't have the power in your relationship it's because you have given it away. Whether it's a man or a dog you want to have drooling and eating out of your hand, the techniques contained in this book are guaranteed to work and make your life easier.

Finally, when I compare men to dogs it is certainly not in a negative way. Dogs and men are my two favourite creatures on this planet and I hope I always have one or both in my life. When you get a good one there is nothing better. I hope this book helps you find, and keep, whatever it is you are looking for.

Claz
x

www.crombiejardine.com